A Teacher's Guide to Roll of Thunder, Hear My Cry

A Teacher's Guide to Roll of Thunder, Hear My Cry

By Greg Slingerland

Upper Canada Press

Copyright © 2016 by Greg Slingerland

All rights reserved. This book or any portion thereof may not be reproduced or used in any manner whatsoever without the express written permission of the publisher except for the use of brief quotations in a book review or scholarly journal.

First Printing: 2016

ISBN 978-1-365-42486-1

Upper Canada Press
St. Catharines, Ontario, Canada

All quotation from *Roll of Thunder, Hear My Cry* are taken from:

Taylor, Mildred D. *Roll of Thunder, Hear My Cry*. Puffin Books, 1991, New York.

Before Reading…

Lead the class through some introductory and cursory questions based on the front cover. You can either lead the discussion or have the students answer the questions together in groups and then present their answers. (Teaching strategy ideas: *think-pair-share, fishbowl discussion, KWL*)

- What does the title of the book tell us about the story?
- Look at the illustrations on the front cover. What can you predict about the story?
- What do you know about Mississippi?
- What do you know about the struggle African Americans went through in the Deep South after the Civil War?
- By looking at the cover, what do you think the setting of the book is?
- What is historical fiction?

Chapter 1

1. *Roll of Thunder, Hear My Cry* is written in a first person perspective. What does this mean? Do you enjoy reading books from this perspective?

2. What is the mood at the start of the novel?

3. Describe the setting of this story. Include at least five details.

4. Who is Little Man? Why do you think he was given that nickname?

5. Why was Stacey especially unhappy about the new school year? How would you feel if you were in his shoes?

6. Why did Papa have to go work for the railroad?

7. The author describes T.J. Avery as "emaciated". What does this mean?

8. What kind of a person is T.J.? Would you like to be friends with T.J.? Explain.

9. Why was Little Man so upset by what was written in the inside cover of the textbook he was given?

In a well-worded paragraph, compare your first day of school to Cassie Logan's first day of school.

Chapter 1 - Answers

1. *Roll of Thunder, Hear My Cry* is written in a first person perspective. What does this mean? Do you enjoy reading books from this perspective?
    a. The first person perspective is when the story is told from the perspective, or viewpoint, of the main character. In this story, the perspective is from Cassie Logan.
2. What is the mood at the start of the novel?
    a. There an unsettled mood at the beginning of the story. The reader senses that a new chapter is beginning in the lives of the Logan family – not only at school, but at home too. Storm clouds seem to be on the horizon. Farming is becoming more difficult, and the land that Papa so dearly wants to pass onto his children is being threatened. There is conflict with the white community and conflict at school. The weather and landscape are dry and dusty – evoking despair.
3. Describe the setting of this story. Include at least five details.
    a. Rural Mississippi
    b. 1933 (Great Depression)
    c. Racism and segregation
    d. Cotton is the main industry
    e. Logan family is poor
    f. The African American schools are not given the same resources and opportunities as the white schools
    g. Life on the whole is very difficult for the African American community, but we can see from the first chapter that there is a strong sense of pride and community.
4. Who is Little Man? Why do you think he was given that nickname?
    a. Little Man is the six year old brother of Cassie. He is not like other kids his age in that he takes pride in his appearance and has a strong sense of dignity. He is proud to be going to school for the first time and makes sure his clothes are kept clean. Little Man has a strong sense of justice, as seen in his anger towards the bus swiping them off the road and the old textbooks with the word 'nigra' written in them. He is given the name Little Man because he acts like an adult in many ways – he can read and write, he dresses with pride, and he seems to wise beyond his years.
5. Why was Stacey especially unhappy about the new school year? How would you feel if you were in his shoes?

    a. Stacey's mom is his teacher this coming year.

6. Why did Papa have to go work for the railroad?
    a. The farm has been losing money for the past three years and doesn't make enough money to cover the mortgage and taxes. Cotton prices keep dropping.
7. The author describes T.J. Avery as "emaciated". What does this mean?
    a. T.J. is thin, and malnourished looking. Poverty and hard living is evident.
8. What kind of a person is T.J.? Would you like to be friends with T.J.? Explain.
    a. T.J. is selfish and only thinks about himself and his own well-being. He blamed his younger brother Claude for his getting caught in a dancing room and let Claude get punished. This is a sign of things to come.
9. Why was Little Man so upset by what was written in the inside cover of the textbook he was given?
    a. Little Man was so upset by what was written in the inside cover of the textbook because the Board of Education had inscribed the word 'nigras' in them to denote that they were for the African American schools. Little Man is angry that the books are old and worn out – the inside page ruins his first day of school. Little Man learns that he is part of a segregated and racist society.

Chapter 2

1. Who is Big Ma? Describe her character.

   _____
   _____
   _____
   _____

2. Who was Mr. L.T. Morrison?

   _____
   _____
   _____
   _____

3. What theory did Cassie have for Papa bringing Mr. Morrison home?

   _____
   _____
   _____
   _____

4. Why didn't Papa want the children going to the Wallace's store?

   _____
   _____
   _____
   _____

Make three predictions about the story. Touch on the Logan family, the Logan land, Mr. Morrison, T.J., or anything else that had piqued your curiosity in the first two chapters.

☞

☞

☞

Using the details found in the chapter, sketch a picture of one of the following:
- Mr. Morrison and Papa coming home
- Logans picking cotton
- Inside of Logans' home

Chapter 2 - Answers

1. Who is Big Ma? Describe her character.
    a. Cassie's grandmother – her dad's mother.
    b. "Clean, smooth skin – was the colour of a pecan shell."
    c. Strong and stern.
2. Who was Mr. L.T. Morrison?
    a. A giant of a man
    b. Worked with Papa
    c. Was fired for getting into a fight with a white man
    d. Was going to work for the Logans
3. What theory did Cassie have for Papa bringing Mr. Morrison home?
    a. To protect the family from the burnings and unrest in that region of Mississippi.
4. Why didn't Papa want the children going to the Wallace's store?
    a. He didn't like the Wallaces
    b. People there were drinking bootlegged liquor, smoking cigarettes, and dancing.
    c. It was a place where an African American could easily find themselves in trouble.
    d. [note] Papa's worry over the Wallace store strongly foreshadows what is to come.

Chapter 3

1. How does the rain make the journey to school more difficult for the Logans?

2. What did Big Ma mean when she said to Little Man, "Now, look here, baby, it ain't the end of the world. Lord, child, don't you know one day the sun'll shine again and you won't get muddy no more?"

3. Do you think it was fair for the Logans to ignore Jeremy and give him the cold shoulder? Explain your answer.

4. Describe how the Logans exacted their revenge on Mr. Grimes.

5. How did the Logans' laughter at what happened to Mr. Grimes turn into misery?

Create a storyboard showing what all happened in chapter three. You have six boxes, so be sure to plan out your six scenes carefully to best reflect the chapter.

Chapter 3

1. How does the rain make the journey to school more difficult for the Logans?
    a. The children have to walk in the rain – either wearing smelly pelts to keep dry or getting drenched.
    b. The Jefferson Davis school bus would deliberately try to splash and spray the Logans with mud.
2. What did Big Ma mean when she said to Little Man, "Now, look here, baby, it ain't the end of the world. Lord, child, don't you know one day the sun'll shine again and you won't get muddy no more?"
    a. Big Ma is pointing to a hopeful future – either in this life (through education, good character, good jobs) or in the life to come when Jesus would make all things new and just (Negro Spirituals).
3. Do you think it was fair for the Logans to ignore Jeremy and give him the cold shoulder? Explain your answer.
4. Describe how the Logans exacted their revenge on Mr. Grimes.
    a. The Logan children dug a trench across the dirt road. The torrential downpour flooded the ditches and disguised the trench for a puddle. Mr. Grimes, seeing the puddle and the Logan children, couldn't resist the temptation of racing through the puddle to splash the Logans. The bus bottomed out and was totalled by the plunge into the trench. The white children had to walk home, much to their dismay and much to the hilarity of the Logan children.
5. How did the Logans' laughter at what happened to Mr. Grimes turn into misery?
    a. Later tha night, after the bus incident, white men were out riding – looking for victims to lynch or burn alive. The children thought it was their fault.

Chapter 4

1. What was bothering Cassie at the beginning of the chapter?

2. In what ways does T.J. try to get the Logan siblings into trouble?

3. What does it mean to be *tarred and feathered*?

4. What do you think T.J. was looking for on Mama's desk?

5. Look up the word irony in the dictionary. Explain how this statement from T.J. is ironic – "Friends gotta trust each other, Stacey, 'cause ain't nothin' like a true friend."

6. Why does Stacey not warm to Mr. Morrison?

7. Why did Stacey and T.J. get into a fight after school?

_____

_____

_____

_____

8. What does Harlan Granger want?

_____

_____

9. Why don't you think Mama whipped her children for disobeying her when they went to the Wallaces' store?

_____

_____

_____

_____

10. Who did the Logans visit? Why was the visit a shock to the children?

_____

_____

_____

_____

11. Why did Mama bring the children to the Berrys?

_____

_____

Character Development	Name	Explanation
I would most likely be friends with…		
I most dislike…		
I would like to read a book about…		

Chapter 4 - Answers

1. What was bothering Cassie at the beginning of the chapter?
    a. Cassie was feeling guilty about the bus episode and the angry white men who were causing terror that night.
2. In what ways does T.J. try to get the Logan siblings into trouble?
    a. T.J. wormed out of work at home and tells the Logan children how they can do the same.
    b. T.J. tries to get Stacey to get the test answers.
    c. He invites them to go with him to the Wallace Store.
    d. T.J. tells Stacey that he shouldn't be a "mama's boy".
3. What does it mean to be *tarred and feathered*?
    a. Scalding hot tar is poured on the person followed by feathers for appearance sake. The hot tar would often be fatal or would cause serious disfigurement and life-long pain.
4. What do you think T.J. was looking for on Mama's desk?
    a. T.J. was looking for the test answers.
5. Look up the word irony in the dictionary. Explain how this statement from T.J. is ironic – "Friends gotta trust each other, Stacey, 'cause ain't nothin' like a true friend."
    a. Irony: "the use of words to convey a meaning that is the opposite of its literal meaning."
    b. T.J. has not been a true friend to anyone. He only ever looks out for himself and is very untrustworthy.
6. Why does Stacey not warm to Mr. Morrison?
    a. Stacey was asked by Papa to take care of the family in his absence – he doesn't need Mr. Morrison to do his job.
7. Why did Stacey and T.J. get into a fight after school?
    a. T.J. cheated on the test and passed his cheat notes to Stacey just as his mom was coming down the aisle. T.J. let Stacey take the blame, even when Stacey got whipped.
8. What does Harlan Granger want?
    a. Big Ma's land.
9. Why don't you think Mama whipped her children for disobeying her when they went to the Wallaces' store?
    a. Mama knew that T.J. had cheated. She probably appreciated that Stacey didn't tattle on T.J.
10. Who did the Logans visit? Why was the visit a shock to the children?
    a. The Logans visited the Berrys.

- b. Mr. Berry had been a victim of a burning by a gang of Wallaces. His appearance was very shocking and disturbing.

11. Why did Mama bring the children to the Berrys?
    - a. Mama wanted to show the children what the Wallaces were capable of and what the Wallaces thought of African Americans. It was best to avoid the Wallaces and their store at all costs.

Chapter 5

1. Why was Cassie unhappy about where Big Ma set-up the wagon? Why couldn't Big Ma move her wagon up with the other wagons?

2. Who was Mr. Jamison?

3. What was T.J. eyeing at the Barnett Mercantile?

4. What made Cassie so angry in the Barnett Mercantile?

5. How did Lillian Jean show cruelty towards Cassie?

☞ Think about and discuss…

Look up the word <u>racism</u> and define it below. Does racism exist today? Where does racism happen and what does it look like? What can be done to stop racism? Can you think of anyone in history who stood up to racism?

Chapter 5 - Answers

1. Why was Cassie unhappy about where Big Ma set-up the wagon? Why couldn't Big Ma move her wagon up with the other wagons?
    a. Cassie was unhappy because the wagon was far away from where the selling would occur. Big Ma couldn't move the wagon up because the white sellers got the prime spots.
2. Who was Mr. Jamison?
    a. Mr. Jamison was a white lawyer from Strawberry who helped the Logans and other African American landowners.
3. What was T.J. eyeing at the Barnett Mercantile?
    a. A pearl-handled handgun.
4. What made Cassie so angry in the Barnett Mercantile?
    a. The white customers were helped before T.J. even though they had been waiting the longest.
    b. Mr. Barnett called Cassie a 'nigger'.
5. How did Lillian Jean show cruelty towards Cassie?
    a. Lillian Jean forces Cassie off of the sidewalk.
    b. She makes Cassie apologise for bumping into her.
    c. Is to be addressed as Miss Lillian Jean.

Chapter 6

1. Why was Cassie angry with Big Ma? Was she right to be angry?

   _____
   _____
   _____
   _____

2. Look up and define the word "naïve". Do you think Cassie is naïve?

   _____
   _____
   _____
   _____

3. What do we learn about Uncle Hammer?

   _____
   _____
   _____
   _____

4. How did the racism and injustice start between the whites and blacks?

   _____
   _____
   _____
   _____

5. Look up the word "chignon". Draw what a chignon is in the box below.

6. What is foreshadowing? Look up the word if you are not sure. What example of foreshadowing is at the end of the end of the chapter?

   _____
   _____
   _____
   _____

Illustrate the scene of Uncle Hammer making the Wallaces back up on Soldier's Bridge. Look in the book for the details needed for your picture.

NAME: _____

Chapter 6 - Answers

1. Why was Cassie angry with Big Ma? Was she right to be angry?
    a. Cassie blamed Big Ma for making her apologise to Lillian Jean.
    b. Cassie thinks Big Ma acted cowardly.
    c. Cassie is focussing her anger on Big Ma, but she should really have put the blame wholly on the Simms.
2. Look up and define the word "naïve". Do you think Cassie is naïve?
    a. "Showing lack of experience or knowledge; being simple and sincere."
    b. Cassie doesn't fully understand the world she lives in and how dangerous it can be for African Americans.
3. What do we learn about Uncle Hammer?
    a. Brother to Papa
    b. Lives far away – up north
    c. Has money
    d. Has a temper; is cool and aloof and impulsive
    e. Served in the war; missing a leg
    f. Proud
4. How did the racism and injustice start between the whites and blacks?
    a. Slavery – the blacks were taken and brought over from Africa. They were treated like animals, or worse, and became people's property.
5. Look up the word "chignon". Draw what a chignon is in the box below.
6. What is foreshadowing? Look up the word if you are not sure. What example of foreshadowing is at the end of the end of the chapter?
    a. Foreshadowing is an element in literature that hints or tells the reader about something that is about to happen in the story.
    b. In this chapter, Hammer speeds across Soldier's Bridge and makes the Wallaces back up. Mama makes the prediction "But one day we'll have to pay for it. Believe me, one day we'll pay."

Chapter 7

1. What did Stacey do with his coat? Why?

2. What was the lesson Uncle Hammer gave Stacey?

3. What Christmas memory did Mr. Morrison share with the family?

4. What did Jeremy Simms bring the family?

5. How is Jeremy different than all the other kids?

6. Why is Harlan Granger so intent on getting the Logan's land?

7. Before leaving, Mr. Jamison said to Papa "The sad thing is, you know in the end you can't beat him or the Wallaces." How does Papa respond?

Chapter 7 - Answers

1. What did Stacey do with his coat? Why?
    a. Stacey gave the coat to T.J. after T.J. teased him about it. T.J. told Stacey that he looked like a preacher. T.J. then conveniently took the coat till Stacey was big enough for it.
2. What was the lesson Uncle Hammer gave Stacey?
    a. It's a tough world where people are trying to take form you or drag you down.
3. What Christmas memory did Mr. Morrison share with the family?
    a. Mr. Morrison told the Logans about how the night men came one Christmas and attacked the Morrison family. They were all killed after a ferocious fight. Mr. Morrison, who was six years old, survived.
4. What did Jeremy Simms bring the family?
    a. Jeremy brought a bagful of nuts.
    b. A wooden flute for Stacey.
5. How is Jeremy different than all the other kids?
    a. Jeremy seems to be the only kid who is unaware of skin colour, or what it means.
6. Why is Harlan Granger so intent on getting the Logan's land?
    a. Before the Civil War, the Grangers owned most of Spokane County. Harlan, who lives in the past, wants the land restored to his family.
7. Before leaving, Mr. Jamison said to Papa "The sad thing is, you know in the end you can't beat him or the Wallaces." How does Papa respond?
    a. "I want these children to know we tried, and what we can't do now, maybe one day they will."

Chapter 8

1. Why was Cassie being so nice to Lillian Jean? What was her plan? Why did Casey take so long to carry out her plan?

2. Why was Cassie astonished by Lillian Jean's bewilderment at Cassie's revenge?

3. Describe T.J.'s betrayal of the Logans.

4. How did T.J.'s reaction to being confronted by the Logan children about what he did to Mama make him look even worse?

5. Why did T.J. betray Mama?

6. At the end of the chapter, T.J. tells the Logans that he doesn't need them or any of his friends at school because he had new friends. Who were these new friends?

Injustice in *Roll of Thunder, Hear My Cry*

There are a lot of people in *Roll of Thunder, Hear My Cry* who have wronged the Logans and others in their community. In the table below, describe how the following people have wronged the Logans or members of the black community. Who in your mind has outraged you the most? Rank them 1-6 (1 being the most unjust).

Character	Wrongs Committed	Rank (1-6)
Harlan Granger		
The Wallaces		
Lillian Jean Simms		
T.J.		
Mr. Grimes		
Mr. Simms		

Chapter 8 - Answers

1. Why was Cassie being so nice to Lillian Jean? What was her plan? Why did Casey take so long to carry out her plan?
    a. Cassie gained Lillian Jean's trust by carrying her books and walking with her. Lillian Jean confided in Cassie and told Cassie all of her secrets. Cassie threatened to tell all of Lillian Jean's friends her secrets if she told her dad about what Cassie did to her.
2. Why was Cassie astonished by Lillian Jean's bewilderment at Cassie's revenge?
    a. Lillian Jean thought Cassie had understood her 'place' and that she was subservient to Lillian Jean. Lillian Jean did not realize it had been a game.
3. Describe T.J.'s betrayal of the Logans.
    a. T.J. told the Wallaces about how Mama had failed T.J., had defaced school textbooks and wasn't teaching the curriculum. T.J. also told the Wallaces that Mrs. Logan was telling their customers to go to Vicksburg or Strawberry for their shopping.
4. How did T.J.'s reaction to being confronted by the Logan children about what he did to Mama make him look even worse?
    a. T.J. blamed Little Willie Wiggins for telling the Wallaces.
    b. T.J. continued to spin his lies.
5. Why did T.J. betray Mama?
    a. He was jealous of the Logans and was angry at Mama for failing him.
6. At the end of the chapter, T.J. tells the Logans that he doesn't need them or any of his friends at school because he had new friends. Who were these new friends?
    a. T.J. had white friends who treated him like a man and were older. T.J. didn't realize that these 'new friends' were really using him.

Chapter 9

Summarize…

In a carefully worded paragraph, summarize chapter nine. Be sure to include the most important details while not getting bogged down in the smaller, secondary details.

Themes

Themes are ideas that are interwoven in a story. They are part of the foundation of the story. There are many themes in the book *Roll of Thunder, Hear My Cry*. Find two examples from the book for each of the themes listed below.

Theme	Example
Injustice	*School bus just for white children*
Pride	
Revenge	
Racism	
Family	
Selfishness	
Selflessness	
Hope	
Trust	
Courage	

Themes - Answers

Here are some suggestions to get the ball rolling – once the students start delving into the themes, they'll find many more great examples.

Theme	Example
Injustice	*School bus just for white children*
	Simms, Wallaces, Harlan Granger, burnings and lynchings.
Pride	Uncle Hammer's car, Stacey's coat, Cassie is ashamed that her mom
	has to put cardboard in her shoes, Little Man on the way to school
Revenge	Cassie and Lillian Jean
	The school bus
Racism	Mr. Simms and Cassie, the Wallaces and the burnings
	The decrepit textbooks given to 'nigras'
Family	Strong family bond, respect for elders, Logans stick together
	Children miss father, father does everything for his children
Selfishness	T.J. embodies selfishness on many different occasions
	Harlan Granger wants the Logan land
Selflessness	Jeremy is a giving person, Father going to the railroad for his family
	Mother going without proper footwear
Hope	The land, the future, the promise of education
	Uncle Hammer gives the Logans a glimpse of another future
Trust	Mr. Jamison, Big Ma, Mama and Papa – all embody trust
	T.J. cannot be trusted – lies, steals, cheats
Courage	Mr. Morrison and Papa, with a broken leg, saving the Averys
	Mama standing up for her children at school

Chapter 10

1. Why didn't Papa want to ask Uncle Hammer about borrowing money?

2. Why does Stacey blame himself for what happened to Papa? Would you blame yourself if you were in Stacey's shoes?

3. What feat of strength did Mr. Morrison accomplish that amazed the Logan children?

4. What is happening with T.J.?

5. Put yourselves in the Logan children's place – would you have accepted Jeremy's invitation to go to his house? Explain your answer.

6. What news did Mr. Morrison bring back from Strawberry?

7. What was a 'revival'?

8. How did Uncle Hammer raise money for the family?

9. Why was T.J. disappointed with his meeting with the Logan children?

Chapter 10

Name: _____

Illustrate this chapters by making a comic strip. Include the most important aspects in six frames. Include dialogue where needed.

Chapter 10

1. Why didn't Papa want to ask Uncle Hammer about borrowing money?
    a. Papa was concerned that Uncle Hammer would come down, lose his temper, and get into a fight with the Wallaces. Papa was afraid Hammer would end up getting hanged.
2. Why does Stacey blame himself for what happened to Papa? Would you blame yourself if you were in Stacey's shoes?
    a. Stacey wasn't able to hold Jack which contributed to Papa's broken leg.
3. What feat of strength did Mr. Morrison accomplish that amazed the Logan children?
    a. Kaleb Wallace blocked the road with his pick-up. Mr. Morrison picked it up and moved it.
4. What is happening with T.J.?
    a. T.J. is hanging around the Simms.
    b. He is suspected of shoplifting.
5. Put yourselves in the Logan children's place – would you have accepted Jeremy's invitation to go to his house? Explain your answer.
    a. Would you feel the need to stick together as a group or reach out to Jeremy despite all of the tension?
6. What news did Mr. Morrison bring back from Strawberry?
    a. The money/credit the Logans owed was due. Harlan Granger pressured the bank and had them force the Logans to pay the amount early before they had a chance to sell their cotton.
7. What was a 'revival'?
    a. A week-long festival of church services that brought the community together. A travelling itinerant preacher would hold the services and picnics would follow. This was the social event of the year.
8. How did Uncle Hammer raise money for the family?
    a. He sold his car.
9. Why was T.J. disappointed with his meeting with the Logan children?
    a. The Logan children were not happy to see him. They were not impressed with his friends and how his new friends were using him.

Chapter 11

The chapter begins with "The night whispered of distant thunder."
- a. Look up the word <u>personification</u> and underline which part of this sentence contains personification.
- b. How is the sound of approaching thunder a hint to the reader?
    - a. To answer this question, look up the word <u>foreshadow</u>.
    - b. _____
    _____

Your turn...

Come up with five discussion questions to share with a group or the class. They should not be yes or no questions, but should spark discussion.

1. _____
_____

2. _____
_____

3. _____
_____

4. _____
_____

5. _____
_____

Chapter 12

1. When Papa grabbed his shotgun on his way out, Mama said "David, not with the shotgun. You can't stop them like that." What do you think she meant?

2. Who started the fire in the cotton fields? Why?

3. Besides saving the Averys, what other positive thing happened while the fire was being fought?

4. After the fire was put out, what news did Mr. Jamison bring?

5. What does Mildred Taylor mean when she writes "I cried for T.J. For T.J. and the land." Why did Cassie cry for T.J.? Why did she cry for the land?

Chapter 12

1. When Papa grabbed his shotgun on his way out, Mama said "David, not with the shotgun. You can't stop them like that." What do you think she meant?
    a. Violence will only lead to more violence.
    b. The Logans and the black community were not as strong/numerous as the richer, white population. Violence would only cause more bloodshed and more oppression.
2. Who started the fire in the cotton fields? Why?
    a. Papa started the fire in order to distract Harlan Granger and the Wallaces, R.W., and Melvin from carrying out their vigilante justice.
3. Besides saving the Averys, what other positive thing happened while the fire was being fought?
    a. Whites and blacks were fighting the fire together.
    b. Papa and Harlan Granger were side by side.
    c. It showed that both sides could work together and had common interests.
4. After the fire was put out, what news did Mr. Jamison bring?
    a. Jim Lee Barnett had did that morning.
    b. T.J. had some broken ribs and a broken arm.
    c. T.J. was in jail and was awaiting trial for the murder of Jim Lee Barnett.
5. What does Mildred Taylor mean when she writes "I cried for T.J. For T.J. and the land." Why did Cassie cry for T.J.? Why did she cry for the land?
    a. Everything had changed. T.J. would no longer be around – he would face a possible hanging.
    b. Innocence had been lost and Cassie mourned the loss of those care-free days of childhood.
    c. With the loss of a quarter of the cotton, a question is left unanswered – what will happen to the land? Will they have enough money to pay the taxes?

Write an Epilogue

Pretend five years have gone by. *Write an epilogue* that will answer some of the question a reader might have at the end of the book. The following questions will help you get started. What has become of the Logan family? Are they still growing cotton? Is Papa still working for the railroad? Does Mama get her teaching job back? What becomes of Mr. Morrison? What will happen to T.J.? Do we hear anymore from Jeremy?

Other books by Greg Slingerland:

A Teacher's Guide to The Hobbit

A Teacher's Guide to I Am David

A Teacher's Guide to A Christmas Carol

A Teacher's Guide to The Joy Luck Club

A Teacher's Guide to The Boy in the Striped Pajamas

A Teacher's Guide to Crispin: The Cross of Lead

Printed in Great Britain
by Amazon